How the
AUTOMOBILE
CHANGED HISTORY

How the
AUTOMOBILE
CHANGED HISTORY

by Diane Bailey

CONTENT CONSULTANT
John Hoard
Associate Research Scientist
University of Michigan

ESSENTIAL LIBRARY OF
INVENTIONS

Essential Library
An Imprint of Abdo Publishing | abdopublishing.com

abdopublishing.com

Published by Abdo Publishing, a division of ABDO, PO Box 398166, Minneapolis, Minnesota 55439. Copyright © 2016 by Abdo Consulting Group, Inc. International copyrights reserved in all countries. No part of this book may be reproduced in any form without written permission from the publisher. Essential Library™ is a trademark and logo of Abdo Publishing.

Printed in the United States of America, North Mankato, Minnesota
052015
092015

Cover Photo: Corbis
Interior Photos: AP Images, 2, 13, 25, 64–65, 84, 88–89; Bettmann/Corbis, 6–7, 40–41, 62; Library of Congress, 10, 18–19, 35; Shutterstock Images, 15, 17, 82–83, 95; AbleStock.com/Thinkstock, 22–23; Dorling Kindersley/Thinkstock, 27; Grogan Photo Company/Library of Congress, 30–31; Caufield & Shook/Library of Congress, 37; Bain News Service/Library of Congress, 38; Russell Lee/Library of Congress, 45; Carol M. Highsmith/Library of Congress, 47; Kevin M. McCarthy/Shutterstock Images, 48; Dennis Hoyne/iStock/Thinkstock, 50; Everett Collection/Shutterstock Images, 52–53; John Vachon/Library of Congress, 57; Teck Siong Ong/Shutterstock Images, 59; 20th Century Fox/Photofest, 61; FPG/Getty Images, 66; Transtock/Corbis, 68; Science & Society Picture Library/Contributor/Getty Images, 70; Paramount Pictures/Photofest, 74 (top); Buena Vista Pictures/Photofest, 74 (bottom); ABC/Photofest, 75 (top); CBS/Photofest, 75 (bottom); Richard Thornton/Shutterstock Images, 76–77; Katsumi Kasahara/AP Images, 87; Mark Hirsch/Getty Images News/Thinkstock, 91; Joel T./iStockphoto, 93; Kyod/AP Images, 99

Editor: Megan Anderson
Series Designer: Craig Hinton

Library of Congress Control Number: 2015930957

Cataloging-in-Publication Data

Bailey, Diane.
How the automobile changed history / Diane Bailey.
    p. cm. -- (Essential library of inventions)
Includes bibliographical references and index.
ISBN 978-1-62403-781-8
1. Automobiles--History--Juvenile literature.   2. Inventions--Juvenile literature.   I. Title.
629.2--dc23

2015930957

CONTENTS

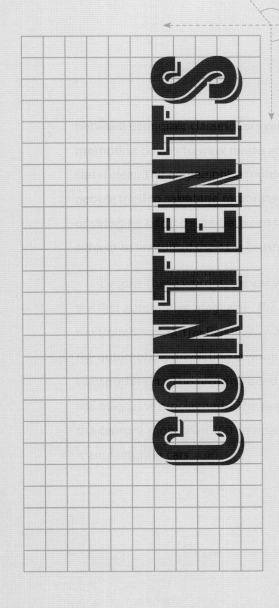

CHAPTER 1

ROAD TRIP

One evening in 1878, Karl Benz and his wife, Bertha, decided to try out the engine Karl had been building. He'd had varying degrees of success. Sometimes the engine worked. Much of the time it didn't. This would be one of the good times. Karl recalled later, "My heart was pounding. I turned the crank. The engine started to go 'put-put-put,' and the music of the future sounded with regular rhythm. We both listened to it run for a full hour."[1]

Over the next few years, the German inventor perfected his engine and built a body to go around it. While there had been other attempts at motorized vehicles over the years, they were really the

Inventor Karl Benz, *left*, and his assistant Josef Brecht drive around in the 1885 Benz motorwagen.

world's earliest hybrids: a traditional horse buggy with a motor attached. But Karl's was the first true automobile: a vehicle that integrated the body and the engine into one comprehensive whole.

But few people in the late 1800s wanted to buy Karl's new invention. His motorized carriage was revolutionary, but it was also strange. No one actually needed an automobile because they already had horses. Not many could afford such a thing even if they wanted it.

Karl's *motorwagen*, as he called it, received a patent in 1886. Karl would eventually be considered one of the primary inventors of the modern car. However, in 1886, the future of the automobile looked bleak. Karl might have given up, but Bertha had other ideas.

Bertha Steals a Car

Bertha, who married Karl in 1872, had long been the driving force behind her husband. It was his mechanical and technical knowledge that led to him patenting critical car parts, including a clutch, water radiator, carburetor, and spark plugs. But it was her indomitable spirit—and knack for promotion—that ultimately got the automobile in motion.

One summer morning in 1888, Bertha loaded up her two teenage sons in Karl's motorwagen without telling her husband. The three took the world's first road trip, driving from Mannheim to Pforzheim, Germany, to visit Bertha's mother. That was the reason Bertha gave for the trip, anyway, although her real motive was probably to promote Karl's automobile. Heads turned as they drove by at the dizzying speed of eight miles per hour (13 kmh).

German police arrested Karl Benz in 1882 for driving a prototype of his automobile in the street.

It took them all day to make the 66-mile (106 km) journey, and it was not an easy ride. Bertha had to stop several times to fix small problems in the car and to buy fuel, which was only sold at pharmacies as a household cleaner. By sunset, though, they reached their destination. Bertha made one last stop, to send a telegram to Karl letting him know they had arrived safely.

Under the Seat

There was no "hood" in the world's first car. Instead, Karl had placed the engine under the seat of the open-air vehicle. In fact, his motorwagen looked less like a modern car and more like an elaborate tricycle, with two wheels in back and a smaller one in front. But although it borrowed from the design of bicycles, it also added the breakthrough technology of an internal combustion engine with three-quarters of one horsepower. The car had a water-cooled radiator to keep the engine from overheating and multiple gears to increase speed and power. Nonetheless, there was room for improvement.

When Bertha returned home to Mannheim, she had several suggestions for Karl. They included putting linings on the brakes to improve their performance and adding another gear for chugging up hills—since the original model required a little pushing from behind.

HOW MUCH IS A HORSEPOWER?

An engine's power is commonly measured in a unit called horsepower. James Watt, a Scottish engineer, developed this measurement in the late 1700s, after doing experiments with horses to see how much they could lift. One horsepower equals the power required to lift 33,000 pounds (15,000 kg) one foot (0.3 m) in one minute. Although the measurement is tied to horses, its power is actually substantially more than a typical horse could sustain over the course of a day. Karl Benz's first engine had three-fourths of one horsepower. Today's car engines routinely have more than 200 horsepower.

Benz's motorwagen looked very different from modern cars.

Karl tinkered with his car, and by 1889 he had come up with another model, the third version. It incorporated Bertha's recommendations and also featured the choice between a folding roof or extra seating. The new model was a hit when the Benzes showed it at the World's Fair in Paris, France, in 1889, and its popularity began to spread. The love affair with the automobile had begun.

Gottlieb Daimler

By 1900, Benz was producing approximately 600 automobiles in a year, and soon other early inventors would push the car's development even further.[2] Gottlieb Daimler was another German inventor who lived near Benz. He had no particular love for driving or cars. Instead, his passion was engines—whatever machine they went on. In 1885, just as Benz was perfecting his motorwagen, Daimler was building his own engine 60 miles (97 km) away with his partner, Wilhelm Maybach. The two envisioned a smaller, more powerful engine. For one thing, it needed to start faster—thus producing more power. For that to happen, it needed a different ignition system. An ignition system lights the fuel to power the engine. Daimler and Maybach experimented with different engine designs, eventually developing one they dubbed "the grandfather clock," because that's what it looked like.[3]

Daimler installed his engine on a bicycle, resulting in the first motorcycle. He later put it on a stagecoach and a boat. Daimler's engines were superior to Benz's, although it was Benz who had first married the engine to the overall

Daimler combined an engine with a bicycle to create the first motorcycle.

FROM TWO WHEELS TO FOUR

Many early car inventors actually got their start working on bicycles, and the designs of the first cars borrowed from the bicycle. They used metal frames, spoked wheels, rubber tires, and a chain system to drive the wheels. Bicycles offered people their first taste of a private mode of transportation that was still capable of handling relatively long distances, whetting their appetites for cars. Bicycles became more common in the second half of the 1800s, which led to an increase in paved roads, signage, traffic rules, and service stations. Early car owners would take advantage of this existing infrastructure.

architecture of a car. The two men never worked together—they never even met—but a combination of both of their accomplishments and innovations laid the groundwork for the modern car.

A New Age

Over the next few decades, automobiles gradually became the norm. At first, they were toys for the rich, but within just a few decades they reached into the lives of ordinary, middle-class people. Drivers have covered trillions of miles since Bertha took her road trip. As automobiles improved and drivers were able to go longer distances, the car spawned highways and suburbs, forever changing the physical appearance of the landscape. The car gave people a new sense of freedom and individualism, with owners customizing their vehicles. The automobile led to the creation of new businesses and impacted music and movies. All of these influences reflected a new car culture. People not only depended on their cars, they also identified with them. While other

The invention of the automobile changed how people got around and allowed them to live farther from city centers.

THE BERTHA BENZ CHALLENGE

In 2008, Germany established a memorial route to mark Bertha Benz's epic journey in 1888. The route draws modern travelers looking to change the future. The "Bertha Benz Challenge" is an event that invites "future-proof vehicles" to travel the route and show off their environmentally friendly features. The cars feature alternative forms of fuel or power and include electric cars and hybrids, as well as vehicles running on natural gas, biofuels, and hydrogen.

inventions also make life easier, few have had the same emotional impact as the automobile. No one names their refrigerator, after all, or gets their washing machine detailed.

Problems arose, of course. By the 1950s, it was becoming apparent automobiles were responsible for increased pollution. Traffic got worse. As speeds got higher and more people crowded onto the roads, the number of injuries and deaths mounted. Despite these serious drawbacks, few people were willing to give up their cars entirely. Cars changed the course of the 1900s, and they will likely continue to steer the direction of the century to come.

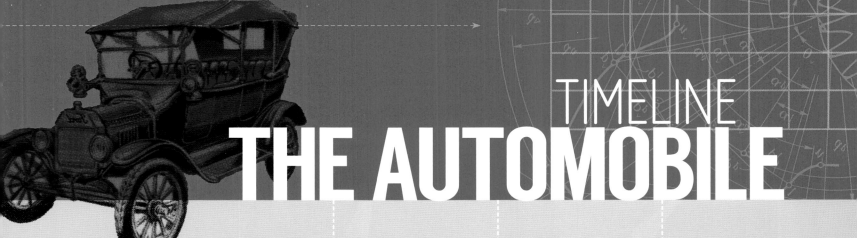

TIMELINE
THE AUTOMOBILE

1876
German inventor Nikolaus Otto builds a working four-stroke engine, which is still the basis for most car engines.

1886
German inventor Karl Benz patents his motorwagen, considered the first modern automobile.

1903
The Michigan Oldsmobile factory makes the first mass-produced car.

1908
American entrepreneur Henry Ford introduces the Model T, which dominates the industry for 20 years; the General Motors (GM) company is formed.

1925
The Chrysler Company is founded, rounding out the "Big Three" US automakers of Ford, GM, and Chrysler.

1929
The stock market crashes, triggering an economic depression that severely affects the United States and much of the world.

1939
World War II begins; a final prototype of the Volkswagen Beetle is introduced; the car later becomes the best-selling car in history.

1942
US auto production ceases so car factories can make materials for World War II.

1950s
The United States experiences what people now call the golden age of the automobile. US-produced cars get larger and more elaborate.

1965
Activist Ralph Nader writes a book on the auto industry, *Unsafe at Any Speed*, which draws attention to safety problems in cars.

1969
The United States introduces the first car pool lane.

1970s
Japan becomes a major player in the world auto market.

1973
An oil embargo imposed by Middle Eastern countries causes severe economic repercussions and causes gas prices to skyrocket.

1997
Toyota becomes the first manufacturer to introduce a mass-market hybrid car.

2009
China becomes the world's largest car market.

CHAPTER 2

THE RIGHT TIME

T hings to do. Places to go. People to see. In the late 1800s, the basic pattern of life wasn't all that different from now. The ways in which people did things, however, changed forever with the advent of the automobile.

Before Cars

Today's car commuters might complain about getting stuck in traffic, but they can still easily travel 20 miles (32 km) in an hour. A century ago, traveling on foot or by horse, that trip would have taken all day, if not longer. Traveling was slow, bumpy, and dirty, and it was best to do as little of it as possible.

The automobile improved upon previous modes of transportation, such as horse-drawn carriages.

STREET SWEEPERS

Thousands of horses walked the streets of major cities in the United States and Europe. And while they didn't spew poisonous gases into the air, they still made a lot of noxious fumes. The average horse produced approximately 20 pounds (9 kg) of manure every day.[1] Street sweepers were hired to try to keep up with the mess, but unsanitary and smelly conditions were still the norm. By the 1890s, city officials and the media were citing the health and economic benefits of automobiles replacing horses. As one writer argued, "It is all a question of dollars and cents, this gasoline or oats proposition."[2]

Cities and towns were designed for pedestrians. The streets were narrow, and houses and businesses were placed close together. Most people didn't travel far to work, or they worked at home or on farms. For longer journeys, people rode horses or hitched horses to a carriage. By the 1800s, public transportation such as trains and trolleys was available in many cities, but the routes were limited. They only went to certain places at certain times. By the last decade of the 1800s, a new form of transportation seemed to be the wave of the future: bicycles. They were fast, and they allowed individuals to choose where and when they went.

The automobile, however, eclipsed even the promise of the bicycle, while solving many of the problems with other forms of transport. Cars made it possible for people to travel exactly where they wanted, exactly when they wanted. Drivers could stop along the way—or not. They could take someone with them—or not. And, eventually, they could travel at record-setting speeds. In 1902, German journalist Otto

Bierbaum wrote, "We don't want to drive past all these beautiful spots at which the timetable hasn't arranged a stop. We want to really travel again, as free men, free to decide, in the free air."[3]

The Industrial Revolution

The Industrial Revolution (1760–1840) paved the way for the birth of the automobile. Throughout the 1800s, the developing world—particularly the United States and parts of Europe—was experiencing tremendous technological growth. The refinement of the steam engine in the early part of the century led to advancements in manufacturing and transportation, including steamboats and trains.

Mechanization, mass production, and the standardization of materials and parts were all hallmarks of the Industrial Revolution, especially as the movement gained momentum in the second half of the 1800s. Faster, automated machines replaced tedious hand labor, and large factories focused on producing huge quantities of identical goods. Meanwhile, this time period also saw scientific achievements in chemistry and physics. Advancements in metalworking, electricity, and the use of petroleum all directly influenced the development and use of the automobile, as well as society in general.

The Industrial Revolution was concentrated in the United States, the United Kingdom, Germany, and France. Not surprisingly, it was people from those countries who built the first cars and launched the modern auto industry. Although the first cars were made in Europe, the United States followed not long after. The country soon dominated the auto industry and largely defined how it developed. A combination of factors put the United States in a prime position to embrace this new invention. Compared with Europe, the country was huge and sprawling, with thousands of relatively unexplored miles stretching into its western regions. Americans needed a way to navigate all this real estate. In addition, because the United States was so much younger than Europe, the country had not developed with the same patterns and infrastructure. Old cities in Europe were crowded with narrow streets, while many US cities were just beginning and could be developed to accommodate automobiles.

Improvements on steam engines during the Industrial Revolution led to new forms of transportation such as the train.

Overall, Americans also had greater incomes than Europeans, and the national wealth was more equitably distributed, producing a larger pool of potential car buyers. Now, all they needed were the cars.

Steam and Electric Power

Benz's motorwagen wasn't the first powered vehicle. In the 1700s and 1800s, multiple inventors experimented with fastening different kinds of engines onto vehicles.

In 1769, French engineer Nicolas Cugnot mounted a steam engine on a vehicle. His contraption weighed two short tons (1.8 metric tons) and was designed to carry heavy loads, but its speed topped out at two miles per hour (3.2 kmh), and it was bulky and difficult to control. In 1771, it crashed into a wall. Despite this rocky beginning, the use of steam to power transportation and industry intrigued other inventors. American inventor Oliver Evans developed and patented a high-pressure steam engine in 1790. British engineer Richard Trevithick later used high-pressure steam to build the first steam railway locomotive in 1803. In the United States, twin brothers Francis and Freelan Stanley also built steam cars. Their popular Stanley Steamers made them the most successful automaker in the United States for a few years during the late 1890s. One of their cars, the Stanley Rocket, set a land speed record for a steam car, reaching 127 miles per hour (204 kmh) in 1906. But the cars were expensive. The $3,950 price was equivalent to approximately $94,000 today.[4]

Stanley Steamers inventors Francis and Freelan Stanley were from Kingfield, Maine.

DIESEL

Sparks are one way to ignite fuel. Another is pressure. German inventor Rudolf Diesel worked in the 1890s to design a different kind of internal combustion engine. Instead of compressing a mix of fuel and air, a diesel engine compresses air only. The compression raises the temperature, at which point fuel is injected into the air and instantly combusts. Diesel engines have better fuel economy, but they do not perform as well in cold climates or at high speeds. The materials available in the 1890s were too primitive to ensure the engines performed reliably. As a result, diesel was not widely used until later in the 1900s.

Electric cars also made an appearance in the late 1800s, but they proved impractical because they were not powerful enough. At the start of the 1900s, electric cars had a road life of approximately 20 miles (32 km) before the battery needed recharging. Both steam and electric cars had drawbacks, but there was a third option—the internal combustion engine.

The Internal Combustion Engine

An internal combustion engine operates by burning fuel, such as gasoline, within a confined space in the engine. A small amount of fuel mixed with air enters a compression chamber, where it is ignited by a spark plug. The resulting explosion produces energy and moves a rod in the engine called a piston. The piston then moves a crankshaft, which turns the wheels and propels the car.

Most internal combustion engines use either a two-stroke or four-stroke cycle. All engines involve four steps. First comes the intake of the fuel-air mix, followed by its compression, then by the combustion of the mixture, and finally the exhaust. In the four-stroke engine, the pistons move once for each step. However, in a two-stroke engine, the steps are combined so the pistons only move twice instead of four times.

Two-stroke engines were simpler to make and more powerful than their successor, the four-stroke engine. However, four-stroke engines had important advantages. They were more reliable, more efficient, and did not wear out as quickly. German Nikolaus Otto built the first engine to use the four-stroke design in 1876, and his invention went on to become the standard for gasoline-powered cars. Despite great improvements made to

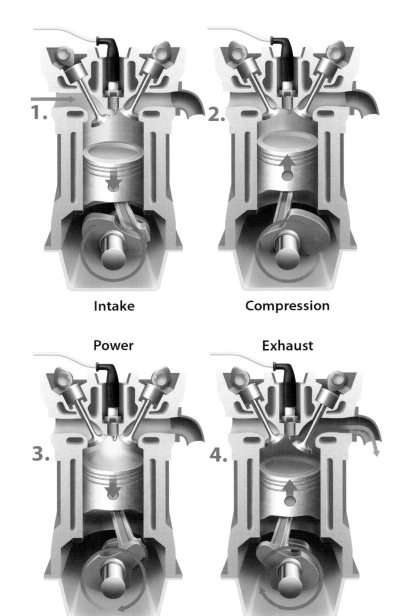

Intake   Compression

Power   Exhaust

Otto Four–Stroke Cycle
1. The engine takes in a mixture of fuel and air. 2. The piston moves up and compresses the mixture, adding power to the explosion. 3. The spark plug ignites the gasoline, driving the piston down. 4. Exhaust leaves through the tailpipe.

engines in the last hundred years, the basic principle of Otto's engine remains unchanged.

At the turn of the century, it was unclear which technology would dominate—steam, electric, or internal combustion. Electric cars were quiet and easy to operate, but they didn't go very far, and the batteries were heavy and unwieldy. Steam cars were noisy, difficult to manage, and prone to freezing. Also, their engines were more suited to continuous operation, rather than the stop-and-go nature of an automobile. Gasoline-powered cars, using internal combustion engines, solved many of these problems. They were efficient and easy to operate. Plus, around the turn of the century, huge new reserves of oil were found in the United States, guaranteeing a ready fuel supply.

No Turning Back

Not everyone welcomed the arrival of the car, however, especially those who could not afford one. Owning a car was a mark of wealth and privilege and proved yet another barrier

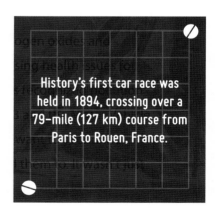

History's first car race was held in 1894, crossing over a 79-mile (127 km) course from Paris to Rouen, France.

between economic classes. Cars were also nuisances. They threw up dirt, prompting drivers to wear masks and goggles and making passersby stand clear. The engine noise frightened horses and other animals. Some people tried to sabotage motorists by putting glass or tacks in the road or stringing barbed wire between trees. Drivers often found themselves subject to lawsuits if their car caused an accident.

Despite these worries, the car was steadily gaining ground. In 1895, the first automotive magazine, *The Horseless Age*, was established in the United States. The first issue was confident about the future of the automobile, predicting it would become the preferred mode of transportation. "The growing needs of our civilization demand it," the magazine proclaimed. "The public believe[s] in it."[5] By the end of the century, more than 100 companies were formed, eager to begin manufacturing cars.

WHIZZ-WAGONS

An earthquake rocked San Francisco, California, in April 1906, trapping thousands of people. Public transportation was immobilized, but private automobiles could still get through the streets. As the *San Francisco Chronicle* reported a few weeks after the disaster, the help automobiles provided in the catastrophe's aftermath helped change public opinion: "Old men in the bread lines who had previously occupied much of their time in supper-table denunciation of the whizz-wagons now have nothing but praise for them."[6] The city's acting fire chief agreed. He sent a telegram to a car manufacturer praising the automobile's ability to navigate the city's steep hills and plow through rubble to reach residents. He wrote, "Have been skeptic about automobiles previous to this great work but now give them my hearty endorsement."[7]

CHAPTER 3

THE BIRTH OF AN
INDUSTRY

In 1901, a fire swept through Ransom Olds's Oldsmobile plant, destroying all of his car models except one: the Curved Dash Olds. With his entire inventory gone, Olds had few options. He decided to devote his efforts to promoting his one surviving car. Olds decided on a radical approach. Rather than assemble the cars individually, he would mass-produce them using an assembly line. Moreover, the car would be affordable, priced at a reasonable $650 (approximately $15,500 today).[1] It was a risky bet for Olds, but it paid off. The car was the United States' first mass-produced vehicle, and the best-selling model in 1903.

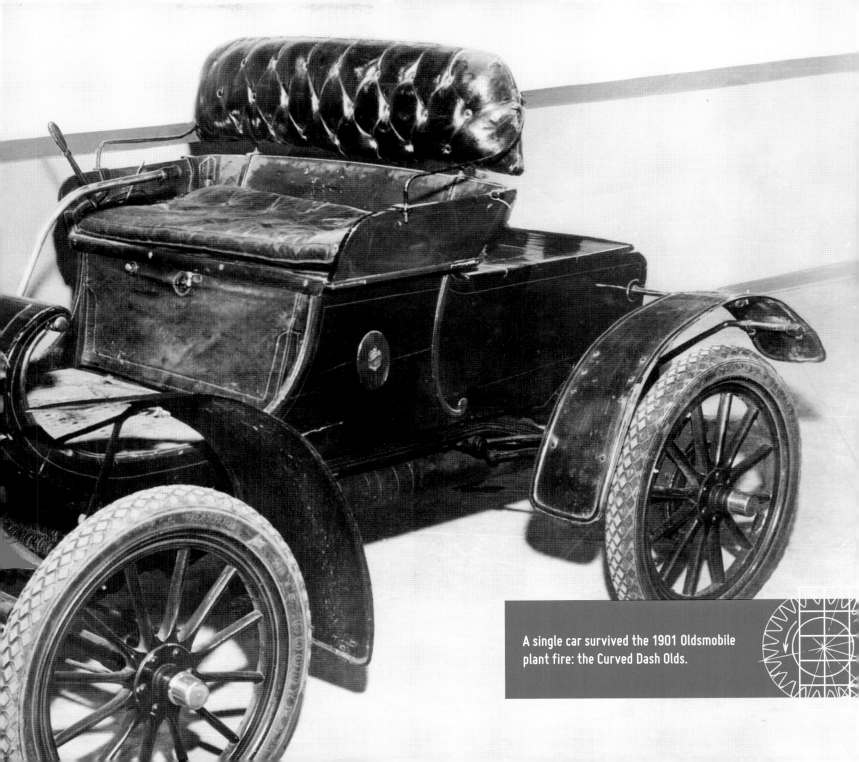

A single car survived the 1901 Oldsmobile plant fire: the Curved Dash Olds.

Henry Ford and the Tin Lizzie

If Ransom Olds saw the potential in mass production, Henry Ford's genius took it to the next level. Ford was one of Olds's competitors in the early 1900s, and like his rival, he envisioned an affordable, mass-produced car.

Ford built several cars in the early 1900s, including the Model N in 1906. It cost only $500 and was a great success.[2] Ford went looking for a new market for his car models. Wealthy, urban dwellers snapped up most automobiles, but Ford believed ordinary farmers would welcome a car if it suited their needs. Raised on a farm, Ford intuitively understood the life of a farmer. He wanted to build a

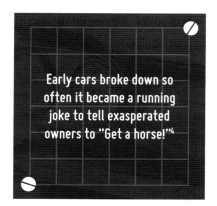

Early cars broke down so often it became a running joke to tell exasperated owners to "Get a horse!"[4]

"farmer's car" that was reliable, could handle rough country terrain, and did not cost a fortune. Ford redesigned his popular Model N with these criteria in mind, and by 1908 he had produced the Model T. It had three speeds, a sturdy suspension system that could take on bumpy roads, enough seats for five people, and a price tag of $825. There were cheaper cars available, and there were better ones, but the Model T hit a sweet spot with its combination of performance and value. Nicknamed the "Tin Lizzie," it became the car that would transform the United States. "Anybody can drive a Ford," Henry assured his potential buyers—and nearly everybody did.[5]

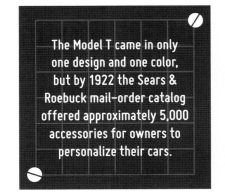

The Model T came in only one design and one color, but by 1922 the Sears & Roebuck mail-order catalog offered approximately 5,000 accessories for owners to personalize their cars.

In the first year of production, Ford sold more than 10,000 Model Ts, sending the company's sales skyrocketing.[6] But he wasn't finished. Over the next few years, Ford found ways to cut production costs and slashed the price of the Model T, making it even more affordable. The Model T was available in only one color: black. Black paint was cheaper and more durable, and it dried the fastest. Within a few years, half of all cars sold worldwide were Model Ts.

The first cars could be difficult and stubborn things to get going. An engine had to be turned via a hand crank, a job that required a good deal of physical strength, especially with larger engines. It was also potentially dangerous. If the sparks to ignite the fuel fired too early, the power would cause the crank to rotate violently backward, and the force could lead to a broken finger or wrist, or potentially worse injuries.

Move Along

Ford had observed how meatpacking plants used assembly lines so workers did not have to move around to the work, and he was impressed by this efficiency. He wanted to achieve the same thing in his own automobile factories. Ford realized his workers would be more efficient if he brought the work to them on a conveyor belt. In 1913, Ford improved on Olds's concept by using conveyor belts to create a moving assembly line at his Michigan plant.

Ford identified several things that would make his assembly line run smoothly. First, the work needed to proceed continuously, to reduce downtime. In addition, the company began using mass-produced, identical parts that were interchangeable on its automobiles. This meant skilled workers who made parts by hand were no longer needed in large numbers. Instead, unskilled workers—who cost less money—could do the job. Finally, Ford divided the work into specialized tasks. Rather than one worker building a car from start to finish, the process was divided so each worker had a specific task repeated

Model Ts roll along an assembly line at Ford's Highland Park, Michigan, plant in 1913.

THE $5 WORKDAY

In 1914, Henry Ford made an announcement that dumbfounded both his employees and his competitors: he was raising his workers' minimum daily wage from $2.34 to $5.00. The idea originated with the company's general manager, James Couzens. Although Ford initially balked at the idea, he eventually agreed with Couzens's reasoning that a higher wage would help to attract and keep better workers. In addition, higher-paid workers would be more likely to afford a car, which was Ford's driving philosophy. As part of the plan, shift times were reduced from nine hours to eight. That allowed Ford to schedule three shifts a day instead of two, increasing productivity. When news got out about Ford's new policy, workers flocked to the plant looking for jobs.

over and over. Ford identified 84 separate things that needed to be done in order to assemble a Model T. Then he called in experts to determine how long each task should take, in what order they should be done, and exactly how the workers should perform them.

The work itself was much more tedious and monotonous, but the new approach led to an astonishing leap in efficiency and production and provided more jobs for unskilled laborers. As Ford tweaked the assembly line production, the amount of time it took to assemble a single car dropped from 12.5 hours to only 1.5, and eventually to a mere 24 seconds.[7] The price of the car dropped. The company's profits on each car fell by more than half, but Ford didn't care. He was making up any losses with increased sales.

The Big Three

The mass production approach—introduced by Olds and perfected by Ford—was all but required to survive in the emerging US automotive

Model Ts wait for delivery inside a 1925 Ford plant.

William Durant established General Motors in 1908.

industry. To maintain a place in the market, manufacturers needed to make a lot of cars quickly and relatively cheaply. Adding to the challenge was that starting a car factory was an expensive proposition. It required large spaces, many workers, and a lot of money from investors to get the whole thing off the ground. In this competitive environment, smaller manufacturers did not survive.

Just as Ford was rolling out the first Model Ts in 1908, businessman William Durant was founding another car company in New Jersey. He called it General Motors, or GM. Many familiar names in car brands were bought out by the GM banner, including Buick, Oldsmobile, and Cadillac. Durant was a salesman through and through. One colleague noted he could "charm the birds from the trees."[8] Durant brought pizzazz and business knowledge to his new venture, shaking up the industry by offering far more variety in GM's products than Ford did. Within the span of a few years, he built GM into a powerful force capable of challenging Ford's dominance.

Coming a little later to the game was Walter Chrysler. After working his way up in the ranks at GM, Chrysler broke off and started his own car company in 1925. Three years later, the firm acquired the Dodge brand, and the company grew to be the third-largest automobile manufacturer in the United States. By the late 1920s, the US car industry had consolidated into three main companies: Ford, Chrysler, and General Motors. Together, they came to be known as the "Big Three," and they would dominate the US auto market, as well as much of the world, well into the 1970s.

CHAPTER 4

THE CAR CULTURE

I f the automobile itself wasn't enough of a marvel, the technological innovations of the early 1900s rapidly improved the driving experience. Charles Kettering's invention of the electric starter in 1911 eventually replaced the hand crank, while electric lights made fire-prone lanterns obsolete. Windshield wipers fought off rain. Spare wheels and rubber tires also came on the scene. In 1902, the first speedometer reported the car's speed, as long as it was between zero and 35 miles per hour (56 kmh). Meanwhile, pound for pound, engines were improving, shedding weight even as they added more horsepower. Each year brought

From left to right: Electric starter coinventor Charles Kettering looks over his innovation with auto executives Alfred P. Sloan Jr. and Nicholas Dreystadt.

A BAD SOLUTION

When fuel is compressed in an engine, it sometimes ignites too soon, which creates a knocking sound in the engine. In the early 1920s, GM found adding lead to gasoline solved the problem. Lead is extremely toxic, though, and its effects were soon apparent. Men who worked at the factories suffered severe mental and physical deterioration. Some even died. Initial investigations confirmed the dangers of lead, and some cities banned it. However, in 1926 a federal investigation—heavily influenced by an industry reluctant to quit using lead—concluded lead was safe if properly handled. It took until 1986 for lead to be banned from gasoline in the United States.

something new, and with each purchase consumers cemented the relationship with their new best friend—the car.

New Is Better

Model Ts could be temperamental, but overall they were dependable cars. They might take a while to start, and they might break down now and then, but they could always be fixed. Henry Ford was proud he'd created a quality product that didn't need a replacement. But there was one problem. By the 1920s, the Model T looked old and dated. It was, quite frankly, a little dull, and GM executive Alfred P. Sloan Jr. knew it.

When Sloan took over the management of GM in 1923, he began looking for ways to give the people what they wanted. He sought to make not one model but many, "a car for every purse and purpose."[1] GM started turning out new models every year—even if there was nothing wrong with the old ones. The cars might get a minor facelift or a major overhaul, but they were always different in some way. And they came in multiple colors to appeal to people potentially tiring of the unending line of black Ford cars. Sloan established a new department, the Art and Color Section, for GM in 1927—later renamed the Styling Section—and under his guidance, GM's cars became more than simply utilitarian. They were also prized possessions reflective of their owners' personalities and tastes.

Sloan described his strategy as a "constant upgrading of product."[2] Others called it planned obsolescence. Whatever the term, it was a deliberate move to make cars become out-of-date—or at least seem that way—so people would buy new ones. It was expensive for GM to constantly produce new models and spruce up old ones, but it helped establish the car as a disposable object and solidified the continuing health of the auto industry.

Other manufacturers followed suit. Even Ford had to change and adapt with the times. The company began offering styling updates to

BUYING "ON TIME"

In the early years of the 1900s, many people were suspicious of buying on credit, with money lent by banks used to purchase luxury items such as cars. Ford refused to allow anyone to purchase his cars on credit, putting them out of reach for those who could not scrape up the cash. His competitors at GM saw an opportunity. The company allowed customers to buy a car "on time," meaning they could pay it off in regular installments. This gave GM an important advantage in the car market and helped solidify the credit-based economy. By 1925, approximately 75 percent of cars in the United States were sold on credit.

its beloved Model T. The company eventually had to discontinue it in 1927 because it was no longer competitive in the market. Overall, the message automakers sent in their advertising and promotions was "New and Improved." The savvy consumer who wished to make a statement would have to keep upgrading to stay on the cutting edge.

Infrastructure

A huge issue facing the country at the time of this expansion was infrastructure, especially roads. The US road system was limited and primitive, and paved roads were practically nonexistent outside of cities. But the automobile was clearly not going away. Something had to be done to keep the cars moving.

In 1916, the United States implemented the Federal Aid Road Act. It devoted money to improving many rural roads—specifically, any one over which mail was delivered. In 1921, the Federal Highway Act authorized federal funds to help build an interstate highway system crisscrossing the whole country. Road construction proved to be a complex and daunting task, as planners sought ways to increase traffic flow and balance safety issues. New streets had more lanes that were also wider. Some highways were designated as limited access—meaning cars could only enter and exit at a few places—to speed things up. Overpasses and cloverleafs reduced traffic at busy intersections by minimizing cars having to cross each other's paths.

The first traffic light was installed in Cleveland, Ohio, in 1914. It had just two settings, red for stop and green for go. A few years later, in 1920, a yellow light was added in the middle to warn drivers the light was about to change. European countries added their first traffic lights in 1923.

The first decades of the 1900s also saw the establishment of gas stations across the United States and Europe. Early drivers had to plan ahead, buy their gas in advance, and then carry it with

Traffic lights were one method of controlling increasing traffic flow as the automobile grew in popularity.

them in the car. By the late 1920s, however, roadside gas stations made this chore unnecessary. Ultimately, as the car culture took off, the gas station mushroomed into a multipurpose business, offering not only gas but also mechanical assistance for stranded motorists, food, and other supplies.

The Driving Life

The automobile was becoming an accepted reality by the 1920s. More and more people used cars to commute to work and to school, to travel from rural farms to town and back, or just to take a Sunday afternoon drive in the country. The number of licensed drivers reached 23 million by the end of the decade.[5]

A car culture was developing, especially in the United States. The automobile was the easiest and most convenient way to travel, and in many cases the cheapest. An entire family could pile into a car and use the same amount of gas, rather than pay individual fares on a train. Even more than that, the car

Gas stations similar to this one on Route 66 in Hackberry, Arizona, started popping up along highways in the United States and Europe.

brought a new sense of freedom and individualism. Vacations began with a car trip, as families hit the road toward national parks and other landmarks.

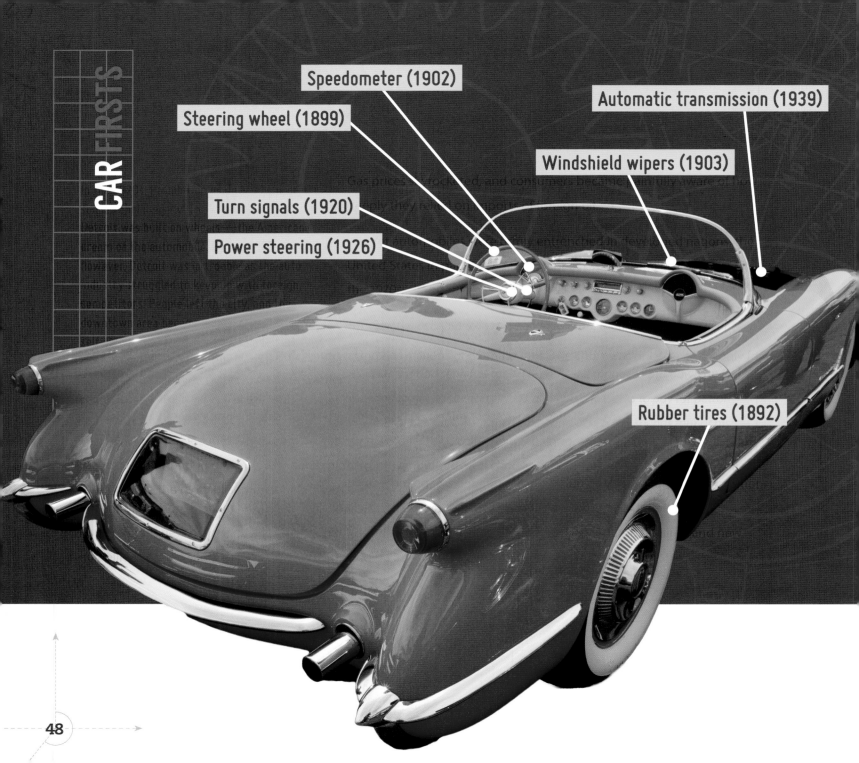

Speedometer (1902)

Steering wheel (1899)

Automatic transmission (1939)

Windshield wipers (1903)

Turn signals (1920)

Power steering (1926)

Rubber tires (1892)

To serve the new traffic, businesses sprang up along the miles of roads during the 1920s. Mom-and-pop diners served meals to hungry travelers, outdoor campsites offered places to sleep, and motels offered a new form of lodging. A word formed from "motor" and "hotel," these establishments specifically catered to drivers with rooms opening directly on the parking lot, allowing visitors to park outside the doors to their rooms and not walk through a central lobby.

Eventually, chain businesses took hold. A restaurant or hotel would open the same business in several locations under the same name. Holiday Inn and Howard Johnson's were two early chains that appealed to travelers because of the consistency they offered compared with nonchains. Travelers knew they could stop at any motel in the chain and expect the same quality. Later, the fast-food industry came to define the character of roadside restaurants. Fast-food restaurants depended on automobile traffic, and they did everything they could to cater to that market. Restaurants began using carhops, or servers who brought the food to the customer in the car, rather than making the patron enter the restaurant. Carhops were soon strapping on roller skates to cut down on their window-to-window travel time. Some restaurants today still use carhops. Later, drive-through windows allowed drivers to order and receive their food and

McDonald's opened its first drive-through window in 1975, near an Arizona military base, because soldiers wearing fatigues were not allowed to get out of their cars.

drinks without having to park. As drivers began eating and drinking on the go, auto manufacturers introduced cup holders.

Drive-ups, drive-ins, and drive-throughs did not begin and end with restaurants. By the time the drive-through culture reached its peak in the 1950s, there were also drive-up churches, chapels, and funeral homes. The drive-in movie theater became especially popular. It was the perfect outing for families with young children who needed some low-key entertainment, as well as a social gathering place for teenagers and couples.

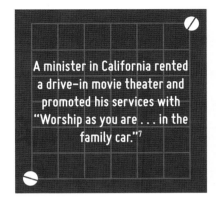

A minister in California rented a drive-in movie theater and promoted his services with "Worship as you are . . . in the family car."[7]

The popularity of the automobile created new subindustries such as drive-up restaurants.

CHAPTER 5

FROM CITIES TO SUBURBS

Wherever the automobile went, it fundamentally changed how people lived. Millions of cars changed the landscape itself as flashy billboards popped up and roads wrapped around the country.

Together and Apart

Before they had access to automobiles, people who lived in the country often had little contact with city residents. A trip of several miles or more was impractical to make very often without a good reason. Because they lived far away from urban centers, rural residents had much less access to services their city neighbors

The automobile offered many families a way to escape the city.

MIDDLETOWN

In the 1920s, a husband-and-wife team of sociologists, Robert and Helen Lynd, conducted a study in Muncie, Indiana. They gave it the fictional name of "Middletown" and depicted it as a typical US small town. While conducting research there, the Lynds found car ownership was so important to residents they were willing to go into debt to own one, and in some cases would sacrifice food and clothing to keep up with payments. The car also changed how the town's citizens spent their leisure time, with some admitting they opted to skip church on Sunday morning so they could take a drive instead.

enjoyed. If shopping existed at all, it was likely limited to a small general store. Medical care meant depending on a country doctor to make house calls, if one even lived in the area. Doctors were early adopters of the automobile, as it made doing their rounds faster and easier. Social and cultural activities also took on a different character. In many ways, rural dwellers were isolated. Some of them liked it that way, but others longed for the amenities the cities offered.

With the introduction of the automobile, rural residents could now travel to the city to go to stores, hospitals, or libraries. Farmers could bring their products to the city to sell. Children piled into school buses, which carried them longer distances to larger and better-equipped schools. Rural

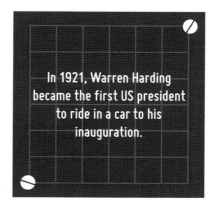

In 1921, Warren Harding became the first US president to ride in a car to his inauguration.

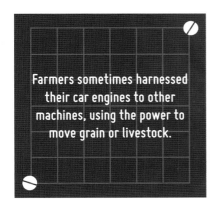

Farmers sometimes harnessed their car engines to other machines, using the power to move grain or livestock.

mail service improved. Time and distance were no longer the constraints they had been. Many believed the automobile brought families closer together and encouraged strong morals. E. C. Stokes, the former governor of New Jersey, said in 1921, "If every family in the land possessed an automobile, family ties would be closer and many of the problems of social unrest would be happily resolved. . . . The automobile is one of the country's best ministers and best preachers."[1]

There were drawbacks, however. The switch from horses to tractors had a dramatic impact on farm life. It resulted in higher costs for machinery, which drove some farmers into debt. It also put many workers out of their jobs. In addition, young people especially were drawn to the promises of the big city, and many left their farms permanently to find a better life in an urban center.

The Rise of the Suburbs

Just as the car brought rural residents to the city, the opposite was also true. Urban residents could easily leave the confines of the city. At first, this was for an afternoon drive or a weekend in the country. But soon, many left

LOS ANGELES

Los Angeles, California, was one of the biggest cities in the United States, or not one at all, depending on how you looked at it. LA became a national symbol of how cities could lose themselves to suburbs. The greater LA community was actually a collection of smaller cities tied together by highways or freeways. In his 1925 book, *Americana*, writer Aldous Huxley called LA "nineteen suburbs in search of a metropolis."[2] The region became infamous for traffic, smog, and being unfriendly to pedestrians.

permanently to take up residence on the outskirts of town. Cities were dirty, expensive, and crowded, and the car offered an escape.

By the 1920s, new developments were going up outside many city centers. These "suburbs" began primarily as residential areas but then added in shopping and businesses. Eventually, these suburbs became self-sufficient and did not depend on the neighboring cities from which they had come. Suburbs arose throughout developed areas in Europe, as well, but their main impact was in the United States, with its vast areas of undeveloped land and widely available cars. Between the 1920s and the 1960s, millions of Americans moved to the suburbs, where life was entirely dependent on the car. People embarked on longer commutes to get to work, and entire subindustries such as trucking developed to deliver basic goods to people living miles from city centers. Companies such as the United Parcel Service (UPS) developed new services as suburbs continued growing.

The trucking industry grew with an evolving network of roads.

The houses in these suburbs took on a distinct character as well. They were larger and farther apart than the small houses and apartments in inner cities, and yards buffered them from their neighbors. And of course, they were designed to accommodate the family car. At first,

KEEP ON TRUCKING

Before automobiles took over the roads, merchandise was transported primarily by train or by animal. Trains could go long distances and carry a lot, but it fell to horses, mules, or oxen to make the long haul over dirt roads—or no roads at all. By the 1920s, the road system was vastly improving, and trucks began to appear. They offered a much larger carrying capacity while still being flexible enough to reach local points. Trucking increased dramatically when trucks were pressed into service during World War II, and the industry fully took off in the 1950s as trucks got bigger and faster and were able to carry larger loads for longer distances.

the garage was located at the back of the house, but eventually it moved front and center, with a paved driveway that connected the street to the garage and the house. Electric, remote-controlled garage door openers became widespread after World War II, eliminating the need to actually get out of the car to open the garage door. People could enter and exit the home without ever having to encounter their neighbors. The car brought society full circle: first it helped connect rural populations to other people, and then it cut them off, removing natural opportunities to mix in the community.

Hard Times

The US stock market crashed in 1929. As a result, the Great Depression engulfed the United States and much of the rest of the world in the 1930s. But the auto industry still hung on, in part because the car remained a lifeline for people who had little else. In his Pulitzer Prize–winning novel, *The Grapes of Wrath*, American John Steinbeck told the story of the Joad family from Oklahoma, who packed up all of their possessions and set out on the road in their 1926 Hudson Super Six Sedan. The film version of the book premiered in 1940. Steinbeck made famous the plight of desperately poor people who piled into their cars and traveled thousands of miles looking for a better life. The car was one possession people kept when they sold everything else.

Garages became common as more people moved to the suburbs.

UNITED WE STAND

Few automobile workers were members of labor unions before the 1930s. That changed with the formation of the United Automobile Workers (UAW) in 1935. By forming a union, workers could stick together as they demanded certain conditions from their employers, such as pay rates and limitations on the number of hours worked. The UAW flexed its muscles in 1936 and 1937 with a sit-down strike at the GM factory in Flint, Michigan, that lasted a month and a half. Employees occupied the plant but refused to work. Finally, GM settled with the workers, setting a precedent for Chrysler and Ford to follow suit. The strike helped establish the UAW as one of the most powerful unions in the country.

Then came World War II (1939–1945). The war effort imposed strict rationing on Americans, limiting them to two gallons (7.6 L) of gas per week. In *No Ordinary Time*, historian Doris Kearns Goodwin wrote of life during the war, "Citizens learned to walk again. Car pools multiplied, milk deliveries were cut from twice a day, and auto deaths fell dramatically."[3]

The United States joined the war in 1941, and by the next year, American car factories were no longer making cars. Instead, manufacturers were pressed into service for the war, and they redirected their efforts toward producing aircraft and weapons to be shipped overseas to help the Allied forces. In Europe, where the war was physically being fought, car manufacturers also contributed to the war effort, but they had to be more creative. In England, factories were concealed in remote areas so they would be less likely to be targeted by enemy bombs.[4]

The Grapes of Wrath depicts one family's struggle during the Great Depression, with the automobile at the center.

Years of war decimated Europe. It was in ruins physically, financially, and psychologically. Its economic infrastructure had crumbled, and it took years for the auto industries in the United Kingdom, France, and Italy to recover. The United States, on the other hand, fared much better. The war jump-started the nation's economy, and in peacetime, Americans were eager to upgrade their lifestyles. By the time the war ended in 1945, it had been nearly 20 years since the last Model T rolled off Ford's assembly line, yet many of them still struggled along on the growing US road network. A new era of peace would clear out the aging vehicles and replace them with shiny new models. Some 15 million cars were sold in the first five years after the war, and by the 1950s, the golden age of the automobile had begun.

UAW workers gather outside the General Motors plant in Detroit, Michigan, during a 1937 strike.

CHAPTER 6

THE AGE OF
CHROME

World War II ended in 1945, but its effects were everywhere. Families in the United States enjoyed a new affluence, while Europe struggled under poorer conditions. After the war, styles of American and European cars sharply diverged, with European cars becoming more compact and unobtrusive as the United States took the opposite road, building larger and flashier cars.

In 1948, the man in charge of styling at GM, Harley Earl, put small, decorative "fins" on the back of that year's Cadillac to create a shelter for the car's taillights. His inspiration, he said, had come

A removable top was standard on the 1955 Ford Thunderbird two-seater.

from the design of a fighter plane in the war, the P-38. Tail fins caught on and began to appear on other cars. They were purely decorative, with no practical purpose at all, and went out of style after the 1950s. But they became a symbol for a new kind of car and a new lifestyle, as their popularity coincided with the heyday of the American car culture. It was the golden age, the age of chrome, the glory decade of American cars.

With a variety of colors and styling both elaborate and futuristic, the cars that rolled off Detroit's assembly lines in the 1950s were longer, lower, and bigger. They didn't just look pretty, either. They were also solid under the hood, becoming more powerful and dependable. But all this came with a trade-off, as this generation of cars guzzled gas like nothing before. But Americans accepted it, because government policies kept gas prices low compared to prices in Europe and Japan. This was one reason US cars were large compared with those manufactured in other countries.

Hot Rods

Cars freed up American youth, giving them mobility never before experienced. Young men, especially, came to identify with the freedom and power driving gave them, and by the late 1940s, a fringe culture of racing had started developing. In particular, these "hot-rodders" snapped up old Ford models from the 1930s and early 1940s, because they didn't cost much and had powerful V-8 engines under the hoods. Drivers made improvements, tricked them out, and then lined them up, fender to fender, to drag race—often illegally—down the road.

Classic cars such as this 1964 Ford Mustang eventually became collector's items.

Hot-rodders made creative improvements to older cars such as this 1938 Studebaker Coupe.

At first, car manufacturers in Detroit didn't know what to make of this trend, but eventually they recognized the young men represented a significant market share. Italy already made powerful and expensive sports cars, but those were out of reach for most Americans. Detroit's answer to this was the American muscle car.

One of the first offerings was GM's 1953 Chevy Corvette, which was pretty but decidedly average for a sports car. Ford followed up in 1955 with the Thunderbird, which was better but still not stellar. The 1963 Corvette Sting Ray shared a name with its predecessor, but it was smaller and faster and looked like its German counterpart, the Porsche 911. By 1964, Detroit had worked out many of the kinks in producing a solid muscle car. That year, within months of one another, GM's Pontiac brand introduced the GTO and Ford came out with the Mustang. These two cars would set the standard for the era of US hot rods, and they paved the way for the Chevy Camaro and Dodge Charger of 1966.

The People's Car

Hot-rodders made up a small but highly dedicated market share. At the other end of the spectrum were the masses—the millions who didn't want to race, didn't care about showing off to their friends or rivals, and probably wanted to spend as little time as possible tinkering with their cars. They were the regular people. And they needed a people's car. In German, the phrase translated to "Volkswagen." So named, German car company Volkswagen did indeed create the first people's car—the VW Beetle—which went on to become the best-selling car in history.

American manufacturers snubbed the little Beetle—at least at first. One Ford executive scoffed, "You call that a car?"[1]

Strangely, the idea of a "people's car" began with a man hated by millions: Germany's fascist dictator, Adolf Hitler. Fascinated by cars, in 1934 Hitler contracted German car manufacturer Porsche to make a small, inexpensive car that would be available, affordable, and appropriate for everyone. Hitler insisted it be able to carry four or five people, travel at 62 miles per hour (100 kmh), be fuel efficient, and cost no more than 1,000 German reichsmarks—equal to approximately $360 in 1938.[2] A chilling addition was it should also be war-ready, so a machine gun could be mounted on it. After a few years of development, a final prototype was produced in 1939. By then, however, Europe was on the eve of war.

The idea languished until after the war, but in the late 1940s, it was resurrected. The Volkswagen plant got up and running and was soon producing the little Beetle, with its distinctive dome shape. By the end of 1946, 10,000 cars had rolled off the line. When Hitler

Volkswagen Beetles included a luggage compartment under the front hood.

had envisioned a people's car, he meant the German people. But the Beetle turned out to be a worldwide phenomenon. The first Beetle was exported in 1947, and five years later nearly half of all Beetles were being exported, especially to the United States.

The Beetle had a meteoric rise, with the millionth model coming off the line in 1955. In 1972, it surpassed Ford's Model T as the best-selling car ever. Car historian and author Jonathan Wood called the Beetle "the most enduring passenger car the world has ever known."[3] By the 1960s, Volkswagen had established itself as a heavyweight in the car industry, and the Beetle's successor, the Golf (or the "Rabbit," as it was known in the United States), also became a phenomenal success.

CARCHITECTURE

Iconic American architect Frank Lloyd Wright loved cars—he once walked into a dealership and bought two at once—and intuitively understood and approved of their place in American life. He included garages and carports in his single-family houses long before they were standard, and his most famous project, the Guggenheim Museum in New York City, paid tribute to the automobile with its spiral ramp design. He also designed a utopian city called Broadacre. The city was four square miles (10 sq km), and its residents would all depend on automobiles for transportation.

The Car Enthusiast

Cars began as bold experiments and ingenious inventions, then evolved into a means of transport, and eventually established themselves as status symbols. By the 1950s, they had taken on still another role: sport. Professional racers took to the track while amateurs competed on country roads or deserted city streets. Racing was a competitive sport,

NASCAR

In the 1920s, Prohibition made alcoholic drinks illegal in the United States. But that didn't stop bootleggers, or people who made and sold alcohol illegally. They often supplied customers by driving cars fast enough to evade police. When they weren't racing from the law, they raced each other. Local car races sprang up and remained popular even after Prohibition ended in 1933. In 1948, racing promoter Bill France brought them all under the National Association for Stock Car Auto Racing (NASCAR) banner. NASCAR opened its first racetrack, the Darlington Raceway in Darlington, South Carolina, in 1950. The Daytona International Speedway opened in Daytona Beach, Florida, in 1959, and it held the first Daytona 500 on February 22, 1959. Today, NASCAR holds three large racing series: the Sprint Cup Series, the Xfinity Series, and the Camping World Truck Series.

but also a popular spectator one. Today, auto racing has millions of die-hard fans. The sport was once an arena only for men, but it later opened up to include women.

The car culture was fully mature, and while driving was certainly a large part of it, the love affair with the automobile extended into other areas as well, such as collecting. Collecting, repairing, and restoring automobiles still captures the attention of many, with some of the more ambitious even choosing to construct their own automobiles. And because the rarity of some models drives their prices high, some collectors use cars not only as an item of interest but as a financial investment as well.

Those less daring found excitement in model cars, from "clockwork cars" that operated with a windup mechanism to electric cars that could be directed using a remote control. By the golden age of the 1950s, cars were even marketed to children, both as toys and in the form of operational—but smaller and slower—models. The Kidillac, a play on GM's luxury Cadillac brand, was operated by pedals and introduced in 1950. Later, other manufacturers came up with scaled-down versions of cars that used electricity or gas.

The car culture showed how mainstream the automobile had become. But safety and environmental concerns with automobiles were becoming more and more apparent.

MATCHED UP

In the 1960s, Jack Odell's company made more cars than all the other carmakers put together. They were just smaller. Odell designed the first Matchbox vehicle in 1952 for his daughter Anne to take to school. She liked to take spiders, but her father thought the toy car was a better option. The Matchbox Company was launched in 1953. Within a decade, it was turning out more than 1 million cars each week. With tiny details such as windshield wipers and headlights, they became favorites as both toys and collectibles.

GASOLINE ICONS

The Italian Job (1969)

L ike peanut butter and jelly, Hollywood and cars were meant to go together. Just as Detroit was making a name for itself with cars, another city—Hollywood, California—was making a name for itself with television and movies. By the 1960s and 1970s, movies and television shows had fully tapped into the car culture, using automobiles to help define their main characters and providing high-octane entertainment with fast chases and spectacular crashes—all staged, of course.

The Love Bug (1969)

The 1968 film *Bullitt*, starring Steve McQueen, is often cited as featuring the best car chase scene in movie history. McQueen's character Frank Bullitt takes to the streets of San Francisco, California, in his Ford Mustang. The following year, the movie *The Italian Job* took another approach. It didn't star a high-horsepower muscle car, but rather a spunky trio of Mini Coopers dashing merrily through Turin, Italy—only sometimes sticking to the streets—as they evade the cops. The Mini Coopers might have been cute, but they had nothing on Herbie. In the 1969 movie *The Love Bug*, Herbie is a Volkswagen Beetle that takes on human characteristics as he leads his driver to racing success. The movie was a hit and spawned several sequels.

Batman (1966—1968)

Similar to Herbie, many on-screen cars were characters in themselves. Comic book hero Batman first started getting around in his Batmobile in the early 1940s, and the car made its television debut in 1966. The Ford company had built an experimental concept car called the Futura in 1955. Automobile designer George Barris adapted the car for the new *Batman* television show. The era of supercars continued with KITT, a smart and sensitive car that partners up with driver Michael Knight in the 1980s television show *Knight Rider*.

On the big screen, secret agent James Bond was always recognizable in his signature Aston Martin cars, and by the 1970s and 1980s, iconic cars helped define the lead characters in several television shows as well. Jim Rockford drove a Pontiac Firebird in *The Rockford Files*, the Duke brothers ran from the law in a Dodge Charger named General Lee on *The Dukes of Hazzard*, and Thomas Magnum had a blazing red Ferrari in *Magnum, P. I.* Eventually, the cars were just as identifiable as the main characters.

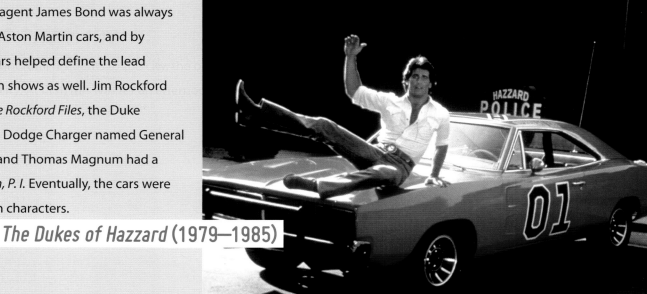

The Dukes of Hazzard (1979—1985)

CHAPTER 7

THE PAST CATCHES UP

"**A** striking fact about the automobile as a technological artifact," writes Brian Ladd in his book *Autophobia*, "is how little it has really changed in the course of the century."[1] Ladd is referring to the car simply as a machine: the parts and processes that make a car. But the car's use in society has changed dramatically in that century. Ladd continues,

> *When cars were rich men's toys, just an occasional roaring nuisance on the city street or country lane, they meant something very different from the floods of vehicles packed onto suburban freeways and parking lots.*[2]

The 1960s-era Chevrolet Corvair is known for its bad safety record.

Cars helped ease the isolation felt by rural populations, but over time they also contributed to fracturing cities and spreading people farther apart into suburbs, a phenomenon many sociologists believe only intensified feelings of isolation. Other problems caused by cars had also been building for decades, and by the 1960s and 1970s, the auto industry had reached a tipping point where the bad was beginning to outweigh the good.

Unsafe at Any Speed

Automobiles came with high costs, and not all of them were monetary. Automobiles take lives. In the United States, automobile-related deaths peaked in 1972, with more than 50,000 fatalities.[3] Traffic accidents mushroomed as more cars poured onto more roads, congestion clogged streets, and speeds increased. Compounding the problem was the relative lack of safety devices in cars, such as air bags. Many cars had seat belts, but they were poorly designed and rarely used.

Some models in the 1950s came with safety measures such as optional seat belts, locks for the doors, and collapsible steering wheels in case of an impact. But these were the exception rather than the rule. Industry executives feared talking about safety would highlight the dangers of driving and scare off customers. Instead, they focused on design changes emphasizing appearance and style.

THE ROAD TO CAR SAFETY

1932
State College High School establishes the first driver education courses in State College, Pennsylvania.

1934
General Motors conducts the first barrier crash tests.

1949
Disc brakes first appear in Chrysler's Crown Imperial.

1959
Volvo installs the first three-point seatbelts.

1973
General Motors installs the first airbags in government vehicles.

1989
The federal government requires automatic occupant protection, including airbags or seatbelts, for the driver's seat of all passenger vehicles.

1990s
Seatbelt compliance increases to 80 percent compared to less than 20 percent in the 1970s.

1998
The federal government requires air bags in all new vehicles.

2005
The legal blood alcohol content (BAC) limit is 0.08 percent in every state.

2007
Washington becomes the first state to ban texting while driving.

In 1965, lawyer Ralph Nader published a book called *Unsafe at Any Speed*. In it, he skewered the auto industry for ignoring statistics that showed mounting road deaths and for failing to incorporate safety into car design. He focused on one car in particular, the Chevy Corvair, although safety problems were certainly not limited to that model. Nader's book proved a catalyst for consumer action. It led to the passage of a 1966 act letting the federal government set and enforce standards for safety on roads and in vehicles, and it resulted in new seat belt laws in almost every state.

Pollution

In 1969, an oil-drilling rig exploded off the coast of Santa Barbara, California, spilling 4 million gallons (15 million L) of oil into the ocean. The disaster focused people's attention on the potential for massive, damaging pollution caused by oil and its primary consumers—automobiles. The spill was not the first sign cars were wreaking havoc on the environment, however. The cars coming out of Detroit in the 1950s and 1960s had big, powerful engines that required a lot of gasoline. They had automatic transmissions, air conditioning, and power steering and windows—all of which sucked up even more gas.

In Southern California, scientists in the 1950s realized the emissions from cars, including nitrogen oxides and hydrocarbons, were accumulating in the air and contributing to the region's smog problem, causing health issues for people, animals, and plants alike. The problem was especially bad in Los Angeles, but authorities recognized pollution was mounting throughout the country. The federal government passed the Clean Air Act in 1963 and the Motor Vehicle Air Pollution Act of 1965 to set standards that limited pollution. Predictably, automakers did not want to spend the money to implement ways to make cars more fuel efficient and cleaner, but the new laws forced them to. It wasn't just emissions that caused pollution, either. From the outset, manufacturing automobiles created pollution as automobile factories devoured huge amounts of energy to operate and produced toxic materials in need of disposal. Meanwhile, at the tail end of the cycle, used batteries and tires piled up in landfills.

Leaded gasoline was another problem. Lead is poisonous and had been added to gasoline for decades because it helped reduce engine knock—a problem caused by fuel burning uncontrollably in the engine. In 1986, the US government outlawed leaded fuel as part of an effort to control exhaust emissions. This had the added benefit of reducing the amount of lead in the air. But massive amounts still remained in the environment.

Although a need for speed lured consumers, prompting them to buy cars with more powerful engines, it came with a price. Driving fast consumes more gas and causes more pollution. In 1974, the United States passed a federal

CAR POOLING

With traffic getting worse around Washington, DC, in 1969, authorities decided to reserve one freeway lane just for buses, since they carried more people per vehicle and could cut down on congestion. More high-occupancy vehicle (HOV) lanes followed the next year in other states. Eventually, many car pool lanes were opened to private cars, too, as long as they had multiple passengers. The United States was the first country to introduce car pool lanes in the mid-1970s, and Canada and Europe followed in the early 1990s.

law limiting highway speeds to 55 miles per hour (89 kmh). However, it wasn't pollution that was the impetus for the law: instead, it was the availability of oil.

Oil Dependence

Lower speeds mean less gas, and less gas means less pollution. But in the early 1970s, reduced pollution was only a fringe benefit. It was the "less gas" part that interested the US government. Political tensions were escalating in the Middle East, which produced most of the world's oil. In 1973, events reached a head, and Middle Eastern countries refused to sell oil to the United States, Japan, and other nations. The embargo was lifted in 1974, but it had far-reaching economic and political repercussions.

LA's skyline illustrated the environmental impacts of cars combined with a large population of motorists.

TROUBLE IN DETROIT

Detroit was built on wheels—the American dream of the automobile. By the 1970s, however, Detroit was in trouble as the auto industry struggled to keep up with foreign competitors. People left the city, and the downtown area became a shell of its former self. Buildings were abandoned and fell into disrepair, and property prices plummeted. Unemployment skyrocketed, and many residents were living in poverty. By 2013, the city was in such deep debt it had to file for bankruptcy.

Gas prices skyrocketed, and consumers became painfully aware of how deeply they relied on imports of foreign oil.

Yet automobiles were firmly entrenched in developed nations, the United States in particular. Austrian philosopher Ivan Illich observed in the 1970s:

> The typical American male devotes more than 1,600 hours a year to his car. He sits in it while it goes and while it stands idling. He parks it and searches for it. He earns the money to put down on it and to meet the monthly installments. He works to pay for petrol [gasoline], tolls, insurance, taxes and tickets. He spends four of his sixteen waking hours on the road or gathering his resources for it.[4]

Becoming less dependent on foreign oil was a daunting proposition, but it looked more manageable than becoming less dependent on the car itself. As a result, the United States implemented new policies to increase fuel efficiency, including the 55-mile-per-hour (89 kmh) speed limit and new guidelines for fuel economy in cars. It also stepped up its efforts to develop domestic sources of oil.

The 1973 oil crisis created shortages in the United States and other countries.

THE OTHER PEOPLE'S CAR

In the early 1980s, Indira Gandhi, the prime minister of India, authorized the country to acquire struggling car company Maruti, which previously had been run by her son. She wanted to give the company enough money and manpower so it could produce small, efficient cars for the growing Indian population. The company signed a deal with Japanese manufacturer Suzuki and went to work making a people's car for the middle class. The first car rolled off the line in 1983, and soon the Maruti dominated Indian roads. Thirty years later, the company makes one car every 12 seconds and claims almost half of the nation's market share.

The Rise of Japan

Compared to Europe and the United States, Japan came late to cars. After World War II, the Japanese auto industry began building cars for its domestic market, but it took until the late 1960s for the country to develop a significant export market. Once it did, however, Japan's influence spread rapidly, and by the mid-1970s the nation was exporting half of the passenger cars it manufactured.

The approach to auto manufacturing in Japan differed drastically from that of its Western counterparts. Japan was a country short on natural resources, such as the metals needed to make cars or the petroleum to operate them. It was also more densely populated. Thus, from the outset, Japanese cars were smaller and more fuel efficient than US cars. But that was exactly what a growing number of Americans wanted. As environmental concerns began increasing among American consumers in the 1960s, Japan was ready to fill a void in the market

Japanese car manufacturers such as Nissan began thriving in the marketplace.

that Detroit was not. Not only were the size and efficiency of Japanese cars attractive for environmental reasons but the cars were also superior in overall quality and competitive in price. Japanese government policy also lowered the value of the yen, the Japanese currency, which made Japanese products cheaper than US products. A different cultural mind-set also governed how cars were made in Japan. While US automakers devoted much effort to developing and distinguishing different models of cars, Japanese manufacturers focused on the overall maker and promoted the integrity of the brand no matter what model was purchased.

By the 1980s, Japan had completely penetrated the US market. The progress of the industry was no longer concentrated within a few hands in Detroit. Instead, the future of the automobile would be a global effort.

CHAPTER 8

THE ROAD AHEAD

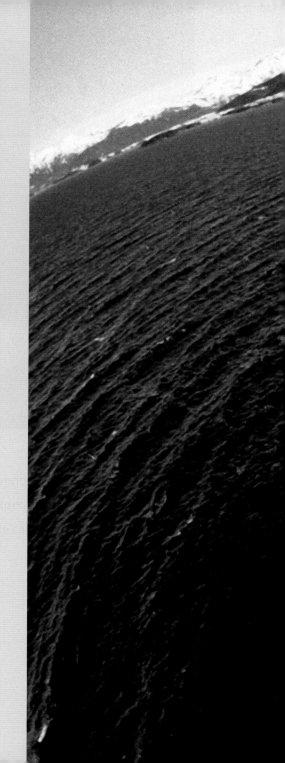

The oil crisis of the 1970s passed, but many people remained concerned over the next decades as they became more aware of the earth's limited petroleum supplies. Maybe they wouldn't expire within a year, or even ten years, but they would run out eventually. The most important question was when these supplies would run out, which led to concern about what people would do then.

Coupled with that were growing environmental problems. News stories reported on global warming. Air and water pollution plagued people all over the world. These troubles weren't caused

Until 2010, the 1989 Exxon *Valdez* oil spill was considered the worst environmental disaster in US history.

entirely by automobiles, but cars certainly played a large part. The general concerns were punctuated by more dramatic events, such as the massive oil spill when the Exxon oil tanker *Valdez* ran aground in 1989 and spilled more than 10 million gallons (38 million L) of oil into the waters off the coast of Alaska. It was the worst environmental disaster in US history until 2010, when an oil-drilling rig exploded in the Gulf of Mexico, spilling more than 200 million gallons (760 million L) of oil into the sensitive environment.

Looking for Alternatives

Cars don't necessarily require gasoline to run. Early automobiles proved other forms of power could be used, including steam or electricity. But gasoline or other liquid fuels such as diesel are the most effective. And, at least up into the early 2000s, they were the most cost-efficient. Then, by about 2004, gas prices began rising steadily. Consumers began feeling the increased cost of fueling their cars and started looking more aggressively beyond the gas pump.

One alternative is biofuels. Biofuels are any kind of fuel made from plants, such as corn or sugarcane. A form of fuel called ethanol can be made from these plants. Ethanol is typically mixed with regular gasoline before being sold to consumers. Some argue it still takes energy to make biofuels, and on balance, they consume more fossil fuels than they replace.[1] Still, the technology has potential. It does take less energy to create many ethanol sources and they also help reduce dependence on foreign oil. Most experts say on average, the ethanol made from corn is carbon neutral with

Ethanol made from corn or sugarcane is becoming a popular fuel alternative.

ALTERNATIVE VEHICLES

An electric vehicle (EV) uses an electric motor instead of an internal combustion engine. A hybrid electric vehicle (HEV) combines the internal combustion system with an electric system. A plug-in hybrid electric vehicle (PHEV) uses batteries that can be recharged by plugging into a power source and contains both an internal combustion engine and electric motor. CO_2 equivalent is a measurement that compares emissions from various greenhouse gases based upon their global warming potential.

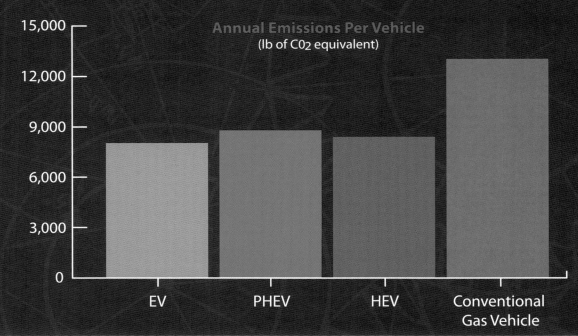

Annual Emissions Per Vehicle
(lb of CO_2 equivalent)

gasoline because the plants used to make ethanol absorb carbon dioxide as they grow. While ethanol and ethanol-gasoline mixtures burn cleaner, they have higher evaporative emissions from fuel tanks and dispensing equipment. Researchers around the globe are also experimenting with ways to use food waste—anything from chocolate to coffee grounds—to turn them into biofuels.

Cars powered by natural gas are another option, although not a new one. Natural gas cars have been around since the 1930s. Although natural gas is still a fossil fuel, in some ways it is preferable to oil. The emissions that come from natural gas–powered cars cause less pollution than gasoline, even while providing good fuel economy. In addition, research indicates there are vast reserves of natural gas that are cheaper to access than oil. Worldwide, there are approximately 15 million natural gas cars on the road, with the largest numbers in the countries of Iran and Pakistan.[3]

Electric cars have also made inroads. Although the internal combustion engine beat out electric cars in the early 1900s, researchers have revisited the technology, prompted by concerns over fuel availability and the environment. The primary drawback to electric cars remains battery life, but improvements have been coming steadily. One solution

By 2015, the Nissan Leaf was the most successful all-electric car.

came in the hybrid car. A hybrid blends two technologies: electric and gasoline. Toyota introduced the Prius, the first mass-market hybrid, in 1997. For shorter trips, the car's battery is sufficient. For longer trips, the engine switches to gasoline when the battery life runs out. All-electric cars received renewed interest in the early 2000s. The Nissan Leaf was released in 2010 and by 2014 was the top-selling highway-ready car. Electric cars can cause emissions, however, unless the electricity is made from clean or renewable energy sources such as water, solar, or wind. They don't provide a perfect solution, but hybrids have shown promise over the last decade, becoming a regular fixture on the roads. Other alternatives of the future include hydrogen and solar cars.

Rethinking the Relationship

Cars aren't perfect, but humans are even less so. Mechanical malfunctions that cause accidents might make the news, but the vast majority of auto accidents result from human error. Missed stop signs,

As of 2015, 44 US states passed laws banning texting while driving.

veering out of a lane, driving too fast into a curve—these are all problems caused by people making poor judgment calls or not paying attention. The advent of cellular phones compounded the problem, adding the distractions of calling and texting to the mix. Many states have severely limited what drivers may legally do on their cell phones while driving.

ADVANCED SAFETY STRATEGIES

It is impossible to completely eliminate human error, but car manufacturers have devised some ingenious strategies to protect their passengers. Most newer cars already come equipped with cruise control—a function that allows the driver to set the speed and have the car maintain that speed automatically. "Adaptive cruise control" takes things a step further. Cameras or sensors on the car will detect if the car is getting too close to another object and automatically slow the car down, even if the driver missed the problem. Other vehicles begin beeping if another car pulls up into the driver's blind spot. A shaking steering wheel will alert drivers if they try to switch lanes without signaling. Parallel parking instills fear in some drivers, but they now have the option of buying a car that will do it for them. More advanced cars can even detect when a driver is not responding at all. In such cases, the car will move itself to the side of the road, stop, and call 911.

While cars can be programmed to respond to different scenarios, they still can't think for themselves. The cars' computers may sense objects in front of them, but they don't always know what to do about them. For example, a test drive of an autonomous car in Washington, DC, showed the car didn't understand the hand gestures of a police officer directing traffic. For complicated situations such as these, the driver still has the option to take over.

Compared with the sleek automobiles and advanced technologies of today, the cars Karl Benz or Henry Ford produced look outdated and somewhat clumsy. They belong in history books and museums. But those early models sparked massive changes in society. It wasn't just how people traveled or how fast, but where and with whom. Automobiles forever changed where people lived, worked, and played.

At first, people were eager to let the automobile restructure their lives, but as problems became more apparent, the focus shifted. The convenience and pleasure of cars was shadowed by deaths and injuries, ever-increasing traffic, and deadly pollution. Yet giving up the automobile entirely is impractical in many places and unthinkable to people who rely on it. Cutting cars out of daily life would require the world be entirely reshaped again, just as it was when the automobile first appeared. It would be a slow and expensive process, if it could happen at all.

Cars likely aren't going away anytime soon, but even with better technologies, neither are the problems they bring. As a result, societies are rethinking their relationship with the automobile, including the use of public transit and biking as alternatives to driving cars. Cars were once agents of change in society. Now, their future depends on how people will change around them.

THE CHINESE MARKET

Although China's political policies discourage foreign influences, in the 1990s its government recognized foreign countries manufactured superior cars. The country began forging partnerships with foreign automakers in Germany, Japan, and the United States to start manufacturing cars in China. By 2010, China produced more than 18 million cars, nearly twice as many as Japan.[4] Meanwhile, Chinese consumers are buying cars at a record rate. The country became the world's largest car market in 2009, and in 2013 its residents bought almost 22 million cars.[5]

THE NEXT
GENERATION: THE HYDROGEN CAR

Oil may be running out, but hydrogen isn't. It's everywhere. Ninety percent of the material in the universe is composed of this simplest of elements. There's enough hydrogen in the sun to keep it shining for another 5 billion years—at which point it's safe to say any civilizations will have moved beyond cars. Until then, however, researchers are looking into ways to use hydrogen to fuel cars.

Few hydrogen cars are on the road yet, although that is changing. Several large manufacturers, including Toyota, Honda, and Hyundai, introduced new models in 2015. A hydrogen car produces power by using a fuel cell. The fuel cell harvests electrons off hydrogen atoms and then ships them over to a converter that produces electricity. The electricity runs a battery that powers the car. One advantage is hydrogen cars produce clean emissions, with water as the only by-product.

Hydrogen cars seem like a great solution, but they have problems, too. Naturally occurring hydrogen is chemically bonded to other things such as water and organic molecules, which need to be processed. This can often result in very high energy costs to produce hydrogen. In their earliest stages of development, hydrogen cars couldn't travel very far. They also tended to freeze in places with cold weather, since the fuel cell technology uses water. Storing hydrogen on a car was another headache. By weight, hydrogen has more energy than gasoline. Unfortunately, it isn't very heavy, and by volume, it has less energy. The hydrogen must be pressurized so more can be pumped on board, which requires complicated, heavy storage tanks. Many of those problems are being addressed. Manufacturers have been working to produce lightweight storage tanks that hold a lot of hydrogen, and some cars can now go 300 to 400 miles (480 to 640 km) between each fueling.

Debuting in 2014, the Toyota Mirai was one of the first hydrogen fuel cell vehicles to be sold commercially.

Another issue is that even though the cars' emissions are clean, the process of obtaining hydrogen, mostly from processing natural gas, does cause pollution. And perhaps the biggest hurdle is the infrastructure needed to support the cars. Hydrogen filling stations are few and far between, and to construct one costs more than $1 million. Nonetheless, hydrogen filling stations are popping up in Europe and in some places in the United States. Plus, the price of the vehicles is coming down. The earliest models cost approximately $1 million apiece. Now, they're relatively affordable—between $50,000–$100,000. As with other new technologies, it may just take a while for consumers to get used to another evolution in the automobile.

DATE OF INVENTION

1886

KEY PLAYERS

▶ German inventors Karl Benz and Gottlieb Daimler experiment with the first gasoline engines in the late 1800s.

▶ American entrepreneur Henry Ford transforms the automotive industry with mass-produced cars and assembly line production.

▶ William Durant and Alfred Sloan make General Motors into a powerful force, while Walter Chrysler heads up the third company in the "Big Three" American automakers.

KEY TECHNOLOGIES

After experiments with steam and electric automobiles, the internal combustion engine becomes the preferred technology for cars. By the mid-1900s, solar cars were being developed. Current advances in technology have created viable markets for electric cars, hybrids, and cars that run on natural gas. Hydrogen cars are also being developed.

EVOLUTION AND UPGRADES

▶ Four-stroke internal combustion engine, 1876

▶ Moving assembly line, 1913

▶ Three-point seatbelts, 1959

▶ Airbags, 1973

▶ Hybrid vehicle, 1997

▶ All-electric vehicle, 2010

▶ Hydrogen vehicle, 2014

IMPACT ON SOCIETY

Growing automobile use in the early 1900s influenced how roads were planned and built and led to more services, such as food and lodging, along the highways. Cities became more spread out and suburbs arose as people could easily travel longer distances. The auto industry pioneered new approaches to manufacturing, particularly with the assembly line. Cars have also contributed to increased pollution and a dependence on fossil fuels, and they have been responsible for millions of deaths.

QUOTE

"My heart was pounding. I turned the crank. The engine started to go 'put-put-put,' and the music of the future sounded with regular rhythm. We both listened to it run for a full hour."

—*Karl Benz*

GLOSSARY

autonomous

Independent, self-sufficient.

crankshaft

The part of a car that converts the linear motion of pistons to a rotary motion that turns the wheels.

diesel

A particular type of internal combustion engine; also the fuel that is used in such engines.

embargo

The act of banning or denying the supply of a product.

emissions

Pollutants or other by-products given off by automobiles or other machines during their operation.

hot rod

A car that has been modified to improve its power and speed.

hybrid

A car that blends electric power with an internal combustion engine.

icon

A person or thing that is easily recognizable and a representative example of its class.

infrastructure

The physical or organizational systems put in place to help a society operate.

patent

A permit issued by a government that grants a person the legal right to use or market an invention, technology, or process.

piston

The part of an engine that moves up and down inside a tube and causes other parts of the engine to move.

planned obsolescence

A business strategy designed to purposely limit the desirability or usefulness of a product.

smog

A combination of smoke and fog in the air.

suburb

A smaller, residential or mixed-use community that arises on the outskirts of a larger city.

utilitarian

Of a strictly practical or useful nature.

ADDITIONAL RESOURCES

SELECTED BIBLIOGRAPHY

Heitmann, John. *The Automobile and American Life*. Jefferson, NC: McFarland, 2009. Print.

Parissien, Steven. *The Life of the Automobile*. New York: St. Martin's, 2013. Print.

Snow, Richard. *I Invented the Modern Age*. New York: Scribner, 2013. Print.

FURTHER READINGS

Car: The Definitive Visual History of the Automobile. London: DK, 2011. Print.

Conley, Robyn. *The Automobile*. New York: Franklin Watts, 2005. Print.

York, M. J. *Henry Ford: Manufacturing Mogul*. Minneapolis: Abdo, 2010. Print.

WEBSITES

To learn more about Essential Library of Inventions, visit **booklinks.abdopublishing.com**. These links are routinely monitored and updated to provide the most current information available.

FOR MORE INFORMATION

For more information on this subject, contact or visit the following organizations:

The Henry Ford Museum

20900 Oakwood Boulevard
Dearborn, MI 48124
313-982-6001
http://www.thehenryford.org

The Henry Ford Museum showcases innovations in the automobile industry through exhibits and artifacts.

Historic Vehicle Association

7960 Cessna Avenue
Gaithersburg, MD 20879
301-407-1911
http://www.historicvehicle.org

The Historic Vehicle Association documents and preserves historically important automobiles in a National Historic Vehicle Register.

National Automobile Museum

10 South Lake Street
Reno, NV 89501-1558
775-333-9300
http://www.automuseum.org

The National Automobile Museum hosts a collection of more than 200 vintage, classic, and special interest automobiles.

SOURCE NOTES

Chapter 1. Road Trip

1. Vaclav Smil. *Creating the Twentieth Century*. Oxford: Oxford UP, 2005. Print. 99.

2. Peter Watson. *The German Genius*. New York: HarperCollins, 2010. Print. 376.

3. "3 April 1885: Daimler Applies for a Patent for His 'Grandfather Clock' Engine." *Daimler AG*. Daimler AG, 3 Mar. 2010. Web. 2 Mar. 2015.

Chapter 2. The Right Time

1. Eric Morris. *From Horse Power to Horsepower. ACCESS Magazine*. ACCESS Magazine, 2007. Web. 2 Mar. 2015.

2. Joel A. Tarr. "Urban Pollution—Many Long Years Ago." *Coalition to Ban Horse-Drawn Carriages*. Coalition to Ban Horse-Drawn Carriages, n.d. Web. 2 Mar. 2015.

3. Winfried Wolf. *Car Mania*. Chicago: Pluto, 1996. Print. 194.

4. Tony Borroz. "June 1, 1849: Stanley Twins Steam into History." *Wired*. Wired, 1 June 2009. Web. 2 Mar. 2015.

5. Vaclav Smil. *Creating the Twentieth Century*. Oxford: Oxford UP, 2005. Print. 123.

6. "Horseless Carriage Days." Museum of American Heritage. *Museum of American Heritage*, n.d. Web. 2 Mar. 2015.

7. "Columbia Cars at San Francisco." *Harper's Weekly* 12 May 1906: 681. *Google Books*. 2 Mar. 2015.

Chapter 3. The Birth of an Industry

1. "Inflation Calculator: Bureau of Labor Statistics." *US Bureau of Labor Statistics*. US Bureau of Labor Statistics, n.d. Web. 2 Mar. 2015.

2. Richard Snow. *I Invented the Modern Age*. New York: Scribner, 2013. Print. 135–136.

3. Richard Wright. "A Brief History of the First 100 Years of the Automobile Industry in the United States." *The Auto Channel*. The Auto Channel, 1996. Web. 2 Mar. 2015.

4. Richard Snow. *I Invented the Modern Age*. New York: Scribner, 2013. Print. 188.

5. Steven Parissien. *The Life of the Automobile*. New York: St. Martin's, 2013. Print. 14.

6. Ibid.

7. "Moving Assembly Line at Ford." *History Channel*. A&E Networks, n.d. Web. 2 Mar. 2015.

8. Richard Wright. "A Brief History of the First 100 Years of the Automobile Industry in the United States." *The Auto Channel*. The Auto Channel, 1996. Web. 2 Mar. 2015.

Chapter 4. The Car Culture

1. James J. Flink. *The Automobile Age.* Cambridge, MA: MIT, 1988. Print. 234.

2. Ibid.

3. David Littlejohn. "Memories of the Mother Road." *Wall Street Journal.* Wall Street Journal, 5 Aug. 2014. Web. 2 Mar. 2015.

4. Ibid.

5. "The Age of the Automobile." *UShistory.org.* Independence Hall Association, n.d. Web. 2 Mar. 2015.

6. "The Burma Shave Phenomenon." *Montgomery College.* Montgomery College, n.d. Web. 2 Mar. 2015.

7. Kenneth T. Jackson. *Crabgrass Frontier.* New York: Oxford UP, 1985. Print. 264.

Chapter 5. From Cities to Suburbs

1. James J. Flink. *The Automobile Age.* Cambridge, MA: MIT, 1988. Print. 158.

2. Adrienne Crew. "Misquoting Dorothy Parker." *LA Observed.* LA Observed, 22 Aug. 2013. Web. 2 Mar. 2015.

3. Jane Holtz Kay. *Asphalt Nation.* New York: Crown Publishers, 1997. Print. 222.

4. Steven Parissien. *The Life of the Automobile.* New York: St. Martin's, 2013. Print. 132.

Chapter 6. The Age of Chrome

1. Richard Wright. "A Brief History of the First 100 Years of the Automobile Industry in the United States." *The Auto Channel*. The Auto Channel, 1996. Web. 2 Mar. 2015.

2. "1934-1936 Volkswagen Beetle." *HowStuffWorks*. HowStuffWorks. Web. 30 Mar. 2015.

3. James J. Flink. *The Automobile Age*. Cambridge, MA: MIT, 1988. Print. 326.

Chapter 7. The Past Catches Up

1. Brian Ladd. *Autophobia*. Chicago: U of Chicago P, 2008. Print. 9.

2. Ibid. 10.

3. "An Analysis of the Significant Decline in Motor Vehicle Fatalities in 2008." *US Department of Transportation*. US Department of Transportation, June 2010. Web. 2 Mar. 2015.

4. Winfried Wolf. *Car Mania*. Chicago: Pluto, 1996. Print. 185.

Chapter 8. The Road Ahead

1. "Biofuels." *National Geographic*. National Geographic, n.d. Web. 2 Mar. 2015.

2. "Emissions from Hybrid and Plug-In Electric Vehicles." *Alternative Fuels Data Center*. US Department of Energy, 21 Jan. 2015. Web. 2 Mar. 2015.

3. "NGV Global 2011 Statistics Show Irrepressible Growth of NGVs." *NGV Global*. NGV Global Knowledgebase, 20 July 2012. Web. 2 Mar. 2015.

4. Steven Parissien. *The Life of the Automobile*. New York: St. Martin's, 2013. Print. 391–392.

5. Bill Savadove. "China's Booming Car Market Is Terrific News for Western Automakers." *Business Insider*. Business Insider, 9 Jan. 2014. Web. 2 Mar. 2015.

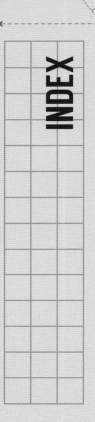

INDEX

About the Author

Diane Bailey has written approximately 40 nonfiction books for teens on topics including sports, celebrities, government, finance, and technology. Her personal favorites are anything to do with history and culture, whether it's the development of dance, the society of ancient Greece, or the history of vampires. Diane also works as a freelance editor. She has two sons and two dogs, and she lives in Kansas.